# ALIGHTING IN TIME

PREVIOUS COLLECTIONS BY THE AUTHOR:

*Cracks in the Ice,* Acumen 1999
*A Sea of Dark Fields,* Hilton House 2000

and from Shoestring Press*:
*At the Edge of Light,* 2003
*North Flight,* 2006
*Poppy in a Storm-struck Field,* 2009
*Listening to Light: New & Selected Poems,* 2014
*The Testimony of the Trees,* 2018
*Brooksong and Shadows,* 2021

\* "the excellent Shoestring Press" – *Times Literary Supplement*

# ALIGHTING IN TIME

*New Poems*

## LYNNE WYCHERLEY

All rights reserved. No part of this work covered by the copyright herein may be reproduced or used in any means – graphic, electronic, or mechanical, including copying, recording, taping, or information storage and retrieval systems – without written permission of the publisher.

Printed by imprintdigital
Upton Pyne, Exeter
imprintdigital.com

Typesetting and cover design by The Book Typesetters
hello@thebooktypesetters.com
07422 598 168
thebooktypesetters.com

Published by Shoestring Press
19 Devonshire Avenue, Beeston, Nottingham, NG9 1BS
(0115) 925 1827
shoestringpress.co.uk

First published 2024
© Copyright (poetry): Lynne Wycherley
© Front cover photograph, 'Spring in Oxford 4' 2009, with grateful thanks to Nick Ansell (Merton 1964)
© Image of reeds p.9/Back cover portrait by Ian Wycherley
© Photograph of Dr Roger Highfield p.27 with grateful thanks to the Warden & Fellows of Merton College, Oxford

The moral right of the author has been asserted.

ISBN 978-1-915553-59-1

# ACKNOWLEDGEMENTS

Warmest thanks to the editors
of the following journals and anthologies for
hosting some of these poems:

Acumen; Agenda; Artemis Poetry;
The Frogmore Papers; The High Window;
The Interpreters House;
The Oxford Magazine; Poetry Worth Hearing;
The Postmaster & Merton Record;
Tears in the Fence

\*

'A Lullaby Remembered' and
'In this Library Fringed with Leaves' featured in
*Thin Places, Sacred Spaces,* ed. Dr Sarah Law
(Amethyst 2024) and 'By the Forty-foot Drain"
in *The Book of Love & Loss* ed. R V Bailey
and June Hall (Belgrave 2014)

\*

With thanks to the Warden & Fellows
of Merton College, Oxford, not least
Drs Steven Gunn, Philip Waller (Emeritus)
and Julia Walworth (Librarian),
along with Julian Reid (Archivist),
Lucille Savin (Head Gardener) and the
wider community of the College
– all notes in the song of time

\*

Most of all, to John Lucas,
lifelong man of letters
and a joy to know

# CONTENTS

## ARC OF LIGHT

| | |
|---|---|
| To a Neutron Star | 3 |
| In a Deserted Garden | 4 |
| A Fern for Christina Rossetti | 5 |
| From a Pore in the Earth She Rises | 6 |
| In Praise of Small Weavers | 7 |
| An Armillary Sundial | 8 |

## A FUGITIVE EDEN

| | |
|---|---|
| A Fenman for a Father | 11 |
| A Lullaby Remembered | 12 |
| Brook Cottage | 13 |
| Child, Fox | 14 |
| Women of the Fens | 15 |
| A Fugitive Eden | 17 |
| 'Hills and Holes' | 18 |
| Fen Road to St Guthlac | 19 |
| My Mother in Moss Agate | 20 |
| By the Forty-Foot Drain | 22 |
| Birth of a Book-Lover | 23 |
| Goodbye Green World | 24 |
| A Life-Spark in Blue | 26 |

## TOUCHSTONES

| | |
|---|---|
| Prologue: A Church off the M40 | 29 |
| i. This Library Fringed with Leaves | 30 |
| ii. A College Carried | 32 |
| iii. Octavo with Unexpected Fauna | 34 |
| iv. As Students Flow | 35 |
| v. The Highfield Room | 36 |
| vi. Soul-Cradle | 37 |
| vii. Annunciation | 38 |

| | |
|---|---|
| viii. Æfensang | 39 |
| ix. Snowflakes | 40 |
| x. Among the Archives | 41 |
| xi. In a Slant of Light | 42 |
| xii. The Garden Graced | 43 |
| Epilogue: Hanami | 44 |

# FARM ON THE RIM

| | |
|---|---|
| As Dawn Feathers the Fields | 47 |
| Thirty Years Since | 50 |
| Vulpine | 51 |
| For the Subpostmasters | 52 |
| Newborn | 53 |
| A Quest for Sunlight | 54 |
| A Prayer for Lost Gardens | 55 |
| Orion at the Doorway | 56 |
| All the Drowned Birds | 57 |
| Out of the Sky | 58 |
| Two Buzzards | 59 |
| Robbie's Violets | 60 |

Arc of Light

# TO A NEUTRON STAR

Who are you,
cold heartbeat?

How many times has your tireless pulse
touched the toiling atom of my life?

In nebulae, your note of snow intones
*'now', 'now'*. Ice-motes in Vela, the Crab.

After the explosion, only you remained,
a small bright face suspended,

angel-child in a ravaged field,
gas clouds hung round you, lit dust,

scarlet and lime – a plerion –
and all the hare-lipped outrush of its bloom.

You flick a feather through our sight-lines,
the jay-blue 'o' of our world

through desert arrays, our upturned eyes
staring from a susurrus of sand

to sense the sleet
of your lonely note –

forever
*'now', 'now'*.

# IN A DESERTED GARDEN

Late frost. How fine
its etchings, fierce.
Light comes in
shatters, sparks.
Is this how angels speak?

Beyond, a lawn
breathes through.
*Scilla siberica.*
Blading the light
with its blue.

# A FERN FOR CHRISTINA ROSSETTI

What curves in glass, a Wardian frame
as if a leaf, as if your life, could fly?

Three-times-pinnate, finer than fine,
its mirror more kind than that hand-glass
you've hidden: Grave's disease, as if
you're all eyes. Tending your mother, confined.

Beauty by addition, how its arc will lead you
on journeys to light, Fibonacci,
while fern-fever walks the west
subtracting my new home in barrows.

They're out there now: the soul-collectors,
biometric cameras, digital maws
more drawn to shop and cityscape than fern.
Let's make our own lens,

you and I: cradle this stipe, this frond,
persimmon dots misted with spores
as if the Breath has breathed them,
all held in lumen, one

numinous skin, a rachis, deftly resile,
for a spine – and then I glimpse you – the girl
the Brotherhood painted, that

signal grace you'd carry, *'filix femina*.
True to your core, run through.

*pinnate* – leaf-blade's divisions
*Wardian frame* – housed indoor ferns
*'filix femina* – Athyrium species, Lady Fern

# FROM A PORE IN THE EARTH SHE RISES

In this borrowed ground we call our garden
a stone with eyes will stir,
ease from sleep to heave
her cold blood from earth's blanket.

Smaller than a hand, her
toad-bones span evolutions,
her swart leather skin, a pouch
of potion bubbling from brown depths.

We haunt her peripheries,
set hoe, set mug, to rest. She blinks
in blue March light, paddles
through grass-cuttings, tea-bags, peel

our rubbish-niche: her hall
to ford the lawn's Atlantic, half-watching us
sway like ghosts at her kingdom's edge.

# IN PRAISE OF SMALL WEAVERS

*Listen:*
*rustle-foot summer,*
*blue Angelus of harebells,*
*barley sketching a blessing*
*on your skin.*

I call to him –
the corn-mouse, building
his boll in quaking stems,
a yeasty snuff
to nest his mated breath.

Scamper-clawed:
his skills could harvest
all our brief suns –
stray quiffs of airy nothing –
weaving us a cradle. Or a bier.

I call to her –
the dormouse, eremite
of leaf-litter, her
solstice suspensions, her
deep-winter drowse.

Sleep maestro!
Tail-over-head, her galaxy
could shelter us
as I would her –
in mist; in must. Ephemera.

*harvest/dormice* – endangered in the UK: dormice (M. avellanarius) are rare

# AN ARMILLARY SUNDIAL
    Merton College

How I love
its little house of light,
annuli of sky, no walls to husk me,

how it holds
solstices delicately, equinoxes,
twin *colures*, and leans

into latitude like a dancer,
deep-inclined, an
angled spine, with all the bulbs

and grass-stems breathing round,
crocus, mauve, mixed daffodils,
a spring sorbet

while its gnomon
writes in shadow, whisper-fine –
for we can bear

only a breath of time –
as stellar mist drifts past us
in veiled rings,

dazzle – Seyferts – helium,
and we look up
from our perching-places –

book, bench,
elation, pain – to
blink back stars. Or sing.


*colures* – principal meridians passing through celestial poles
*Seyfert* – type of galaxy with bright core

# A Fugitive Eden

*for my family in memory*

# A FENMAN FOR A FATHER

The Doppler effects of memory –
you're near, you're far,
fowler – fisher –
a trailing breath,
wry vowels of
Northants-meets-Fens
*that pheasant'll get
'is cum-oopance!*

We'd sit by fraying angels,
orange carpals, my preschool
thumbs surprisingly deft
as we plucked silk,
plucked fire, from
October skin
with feral tenderness,
ruffed an old tin bath.

Rain-fade:
elsewhere you'd wade
through lustre
where moon-trees hover
warily over their twins.
Fenman: no kin
to now – our lives flattened
in zeroes and ones,

click-bait luring
our shallows –
but a weight of water,
roach, bream,
scenting your shins.
Oxygen, its rising Os
a sight to bate our breath.

*click-bait* – enticements to 'click' on lucrative online links

# A LULLABY REMEMBERED

Fey reeds of The Fens, I hear you –
through static, crackle-glaze,
I hear you – the lullaby
you make of the wind,
litany of winter: how your

summered-purple wanes
to white-gold sibilance
that limns and lines the drains
and spirit-lodes, peat fields,
their raven folds, as if

a presence roams there
heaven-fledged, scapulars
of spun platinum moulting wonder
and how – equerry to ditches,
escort to inverted moons –

you make a living song
of the light, and how –
despite all – herbicides,
hurtling roads – you persist;
and how, faith-keeper, your

fine threads reel in my
childhood: that crab-apple house
left dangling too long
off the rim of
the hastening world.

# BROOK COTTAGE

It's still there –
a charcoal smudge, damp thatch
shouldering through tree-light.
Nest among nests, ring-doves.

No idyll. It flooded in summer,
brackish, otter-haired, our
tatters swept in our parents' arms,
their faces daybreak-grey

though doves would sing and soothe,
bees re-weave the doorway,
stray motes of warming magic
as I played with pegs by the floor.

Now years, new-builds, breathe
at its back, hustle it with
strangeness. Can I hear
a brook, lisp-silver, flutter-straw

of Infields Road, thin flotsam
on its string? Dusty
Springfield, the Pogles? Or that
buttercup girl with a
three-stitch smile – knit one

and pearl – as if the brook
still utters, as if I once existed
after all.

*Pogles* – children's TV series created by Oliver Postgate

# CHILD, FOX

The last house shed its petal.
I was tickle-deep in tawny grass
when our orbits crossed

child, Fox. Fox, child

two heartbeats assessing each other
*tan-tan, agogô,*
his luminous eyes

unpeeled from earth, wild amber,
a fathomless touch –
fleeting torch –

that set the fields on fire

before the phones came,
clones, to swallow lives and spit
them out again

*en masse.* The phones. Not a wing,
not even a dead thing
gifting its ooze to the grass.

*tan-tan, agogô* – percussion instruments (Afro-Brazilian/Ghanaian)

# WOMEN OF THE FENS

I search for them: wind-blown figures
on childhood's rim,
brown poppies from long horizons,
heads scarved, boots caked,
sail-cloth poised
to billow on peat seas.

Beet-singlers. Celery pickers.
They'd stitch an eerie nowhere
where living has few
hedgerows, far barns sail
and years unmoor
in distance. Fen gals!

Too little known for legend
who'd clump in shops,
brush past my ears,
petrol-stop, *did you hear
of Sal, them down Mile Drove?*
then laugh – cough – a *tissick*

as if their lungs were burr-sewn
by 'Fen Blows'. *Snatch in
that washing! Latch out
the dust!* as field-clouds
grew mandibular
and all the land a ghost.

Now I too would latch
light against rust, batten
against loss. I see them pitch in
rhythms, bow-to-stern,
newspaper-stuffed
to wad the cold,

sacks at their waist
or lap-plastic flapping
and then those knives –
L-shaped knives –
to hook lime-green from black,
spell *lean, Deep Lode,*

*imperilled* as I'm
riding to Chatteris, squinting
through time, turbine
blades, Fillenham's Drain,
our van rattling and all
the sky blown round,

their sharp shapes
needling memory– for what
can a child have known?
*(she's a rum owd gal*
Nana-Millie would say as I
tickled feint with crayons) –

as they josh, cuss,
jiffy-reef their clothes.
The wind, hopelessly eloquent,
writing its lines
in each face.

## A FUGITIVE EDEN

We'd live by queasy pastorals,
a pleached crossing of time and place

the A1's fray beyond fields,
carriageways hung in tar-simmered air

homeless, faintly howling
and on some winds mauve quanta

of smoke, Fletton to Yaxley,
brickwork to brickworks

that spoke skies with unravelling tongues,
dragon-wisp to dragon

our blessing-cup a wire-ringed copse
ambivalent with nettles

our small heels slurred with leaf-mould
and the shy plosives of berries

as paths parted to sheeny skin
where rain-bugs rowed, skittered

*flick-pause, flick-pause* their oars
inked on a tin-lit page

fanning our world
with fey rings.

## 'HILLS AND HOLES'
### for my brother

Tumbleweed, how we'd
skip and run! Each dell
a novelty, each small
horizon, cup of 'squash,
haplessly sufficient.
Fray Bentos tin, a picnic's

lumpen blanket; Edna's
hair, '60s-bouffant, a magnet
for sly wings. *You tell
your father: we're not
coming here again!* As we
fluttered, ran. Still forming,

how could we selve
those yet-to-name flowers,
Pasque, early orchid,
dark mullein? How delve
the hollows' miracle?
Unspoken stone –

sunlight-made-stone –
hauled to dazzled water,
inky barges sliding to far rims
where transepts grew
to towers, grew to dream.
Trancing. Ely's bloom.

*'Hills and Holes'* – medieval quarry, Barnack, Cambs (now a floral nature reserve), supplied Ely and Peterborough cathedrals

# FEN ROAD TO ST GUTHLAC
### Croyland, Lincolnshire

What has the cold wind taken?

These fields have bled to agri-barns,
fast freight. Palimpsests,
peat to silt and not a face in sight.

No roding-men to clef the breeze,
stave the drains, their
shadows hauling at shadow.

No clayers in their digging-irons,
'witching' blades to
work the dark, graffito.

No, only you remain:
twelve centuries have not slain you,
your thorn stubborn in memory,

cuttle-bone in autumn's throat
as you stand in a breviary
of fish and fowl,

fens carr, water germander
waiting to give council
to fresh kings. Your abbey

gaunt behind you, long-boned ruin,
dripping sheen and solder
after rain, and the once-marsh

lisping. As you gaze –
half shrike, half glebe – into our
gusts, our racing lives. Outpost

of a stillness we have lost.

*roding /witch* – ditch clearing using tall rods; clay-cutting spade (Fens dialect)

# MY MOTHER IN MOSS AGATE

*She'll sing in the kitchen*
*with Tom Jones.*
*Quick, drop the volume!*
*They're home.*

Gifted to you when your waters broke,
its swings out on a sun-strand
as you lean, or nests
unseen in V-necks,
love's peri-green, its
manganese paired with chrome
in random miracles.

*Neil Diamond, Johnny Mathis,*
*Chopping board: how the parings fly!*

Your grandchildren
teeth on it, turn it,
baffled, in starfish hands:
cold on one side, warm
on the other; soul-window
to a selkie life, your seal-song,
mezzo-soprano, rarely aired

*Engelbert's 'Release Me'*
*then Cher, then Marley, then Cream*

while kettle prates, saucepans
steam, rust carotenes pent up
and Ham, Pickle, Egg Mayo –
stratifications of
boredom and wheat –
incant your daily
piece-work for the men.

*Sacha Distel. Did he know*
*how dark-eyed 'Raindrops' dance?*

Now the death you'd
swim through opens its door
to sea-grass, swirls, fractal.
A tilde in the tide,
you'll ripple-drift toward us.
Song carried in
that greater song,

the light reunited
over your head.

*Sacha Distel* – known for 'Raindrops Keep Falling on My Head' (1970; Burt Bacharach/Hal David 1969)

# BY THE FORTY-FOOT DRAIN
### Cambridgeshire Fens

Loneliness. The nail of the wind.
The dyke's antimony
stretching for miles.

A road in suspension,
black fields below,
wheel-tracks ghosting off the edge.

Sometimes I'd hear
stories of fatalities,
grey cats of fog

stalking the fen,
winch-cranes stooping
over fallen metal bodies.

This road reminds me
of times of pain –
taut, uncertain, too tense to sustain –

earth to my left, water to my right,
whether I would drown
in darkness or light.

## BIRTH OF A BOOK-LOVER

It wasn't the deaths that chilled me,
each tiny skull that touched my foot

by Brook Cottage, teeth bared by teeth,
a vole's or a rabbit's, white-pearl

nor even the gibbet I chanced on,
pitiful shadows hung in rows, rank velvet

but the cold, the stealing cold, that
data-speak would usher even then

*bit rates per second, closed-loop control system*
our lives shrunk to *operatives*

grey-bleak, while books – late-found –
were creaturely, rare: chance encounters

by dusty stairs, *Wuthering Heights*,
covers faunal, furled; leaf-tooled;

scent of must or leather; folios' long
bodies lank with cream; lintels

to Arden, lovers, word-streams
where I'd sit by Lorenzo immersed

in *soft stillness of the night*. Love
in love with the universe.

# GOODBYE GREEN WORLD

*I cradle a leaf: it cradles me,*
*skin to cellulose, stoma to pore;*
*mappa mundi, crêpe-satin.*

Rushing by, all the new leaves – how they
bleed beyond glass, windscreens' blur,
adrenalin of unseeing.

*Its midrib, veins; my palm,*
*how cheirology twins us,*
*life-line, heart-line, Mount Luna.*

STAY IN LANE   JUNCTION 10
Hawthorn? spindle? all slurred,
their tender light hard-shouldered,

*Chartreuse in sunlight,*
*tussah to the touch, unveiled*
*by light-microscopy or love.*

The once-grass gone to asphalt, iron –
girders, pylon, bitumen –
under car-roar, under the burn.

*Chlorophyll, lus-an-óir,*
*how it makes a glade in me,*
*a fée of me.*

ALL OTHER ROUTES A1(M)
gantries flashing over us. We're
spurred by signs, new diktats.

*Beryline, wild beauty*
*intimate in a child's hands*
*how bright its cosmos breathes.*

Goodbye my first world,
goodbye my first love,
thorn-buds, eye-bright, willow.

*This leaf: this skin.*
*Filigree, our rivers run,*
*a fount – a breath – love's oxygen.*

*tussah* – wild silk
*lus-an-óir* – hedge-mustard (Irish legacy)

# A LIFE-SPARK IN BLUE

Lark calling down the long light

   how a thousand fragilities
   suspend from your song,
   *molinia*, the heath; this dot
   on a farm; spots of marjoram,
   camphor-meets-thyme; life-crumbs.

Lark calling down the long light

   how our once-world hung, even then,
   cats-cradled from your pin-points,
   my parents, young brother,
   our swatch of grass, and we
   in our ground-nest, peering.

Lark calling, alto-soprano,

   over a school, the maypole
   as we clumped and clattered round,
   no Ruskin perfection, no *fille*
   *mal gardée,* our curled
   fingers clinging to light.

Lark, fuscous, if you should fade

   will we fade too? The fields
   fold their silt, our garden its kite?
   All the green silk? As you
   call from the Red List, little
   litany of blood, your

   trilling heart a boson in blue.

---

*maypole* – Folksworth C of E school (then tiny)  *Ruskin* – May-tide revivalist
*fille mal gardée* – (variant) Frederick Ashton's maypole-dancing ballet

# Touchstones

*Variations from a cycle of poems
inspired by Merton College, Oxford
dedicated to the memory of
Dr Roger Highfield (1922–2017)
history tutor, emeritus Fellow, and librarian*

# PROLOGUE: A CHURCH OFF THE M40

*History, poetry:*
*human frames. You'd*
*sift through facts; I dream.*

Warm stone, old bergamot,
this nave could float
in vernal-grass, in brome.

*'No Wycliffite'* you'd note,
eyes bright, reading
Warden Gilbert

in stained glass: his ferrous
robe, doctor's cap, a
bullfinch in suspension.

Beyond, the road is restless,
carbon-screed.
It cries, it bays –

time's furore,
time swept away.

*Gilbert (Robert)* – Merton College Warden 1417–21; Roger Highfield was interested in Wyclif (Fellow 1356) and the Lollards (with thanks to R B Peberdy)

# i. THIS LIBRARY FRINGED WITH LEAVES
### Merton College

*Library teams: we tread a line*
*between lender and loan,*
*grey borderland where*
*snowferns, kennings, breathe.*

I work
among the lacewings,
windows' lead, slant shadows;
they strengthen, thin;
pizzicato, fits of rain,
window-panes' translucence
run with feint.

Not yet –

don't prune the leaves
just yet. Foliate borders,
fresh, the cinnabar
still drying. Virginia creeper,
heart's fine net, '*Motu Cordis*.

These fascicles,
red cloth. These burnishes,
Morocco. Hegel, Buber,
bowered. Each day
a discourse deepens,
cordovan.

Not yet –

a student in her window seat
as if our souls could curl,
historiated initials,
pigments-made-light,
leaf-veins delicate.

Not yet –

are all our lives stochastic,
rain's slant fall?
Too soon these leaves
and health will fail –
*fast-fade, crackle, white-out, null.*



*'[De] Motu Cordis'* – 1628, seminal work on blood circulation by William Harvey, Warden of Merton College 1645–, whose portrait hung by the Old Warden's Lodgings library, my former workplace

## ii. A COLLEGE CARRIED

*Fox-flecks and must;*
*feel the cloth, new buckram,*
*a frontispiece, thumb-browned;*
*lignin, aromatic, sparse*
*phenols breaking down.*

Then here you are,
J.R.L.H., unique.
That dip of your
head, *'good morning'*.
Smile kindles smile:
unspoken kindness speaks.

Grey eyes, blue-grey,
astute: how carbon tints
in manuscripts give depth.
A hint of mirth
rarely far away, the Effra's
play in Dulwich.

Acumen: how bees
organise so beautifully,
how thoughts; nectar
tested, tethered,
knowledge grown to
honeycombs, Oise-amber.

Sharp heels,
staccato walking stick.
No need for crimson,
formal. Warmth in your wake,
a college carried,
vellum; gall-ink; Latin.

How could it be? Your
labours unimaginable,
space-time curved
through you, Merton's rolls.
*Just this*, you imply, *just this*:
*I was a not-quite-soldier
and I served.*

J.R.L.H. – J.Roger Loxley Highfield, dedicatee, who studied, in youth, in Dulwich *Merton's rolls* – his remarkable work on the College's wealth of 13th-century account rolls was published in 1964 *soldier* (1939–45) – Dr Philip Waller (Emeritus Fellow), who gave a moving address at Roger's memorial service, testifies to his modesty

### iii. OCTAVO WITH UNEXPECTED FAUNA

*Books in, books out, striated.*
*Footings, copestones, thawls;*
*these drystone walls*
*will never be completed*

~

Ghost Winged or Bordered Sallow?
Map Winged or Tawny Wave?
A lone moth's insurrection,
its dusty parchment
cupreous and grey.

~

Lit-crit or Law? Ladybirds:
they spilt from a spine,
free of perjury,
Court of Pleas. Bold beads,

how Emily Dickinson
red-stitched her quires,
folding her brio, fire opals, away.

~

Wasps, tiger-shreds,
head-butting desks;
some days we're wildlife wranglers,
retrieve a sparrow, brown-ruche

or that starling who beat, beat,
no head for Classics.
Jumper-wrapped, it blinked,
swept to a cobalt instant, sublime –

salving its heart,
the ether, and mine.

## iv. AS STUDENTS FLOW

*In they'd flap, our owlets!*
*Ice made floss, fluffed snow.*
*Night eyes semi-startled, ripe to know.*

Term's rush. How life-paths cross,
Brownian motion or pas-de-deux?
Tutors flit past, breathless!
Students. Wild-flower faces,
mercurial smiles,
lamé – moiré – emoji.

Eighth week. What have they left?
Sundry notes, snow-drifts.
Papers, delirious lichen.
Aha! Vintage chocolate,
provenance unknown.

You chuckle. Ever punctual,
pace past. Clock-house,
wainscot, newel…
Card-catalogue, your friend.
It rusticates on the landing,

*opera omnia quae, extant*
while I'm logged in, amphibian
*memberships, accessions…*
*RFID, labels, renewals…*
cave-dive, work-finned.

And now, beyond, trans-global?
How AI hastens, e-life hurls.
Fast-beyond-fast,
'brave new world'. Or *Faust*.

*Owlets* – (students) Old Warden's Lodgings library was known as 'OWL'

## v. THE HIGHFIELD ROOM

*Vowels-on-the-wing, am I*
*passage-migrant, passerine?*
*A satin sky, no perch but in a poem.*

To taste remembered catalogues,
to tongue: 'L' through 'M',
medieval. I'd wade among
the phonemes,
shelve their gleams.

Tomes; wood-grain; handsome.
What can I offer,
time-thinned? I trace a slender
heather-house,
a poem. Rice-paper lantern
in a culling wind.

History; poetry. Distant poles?
Each one's a photocathode,
light-made-new.
Fact or trope? The limpid soul's
subjective and yet true.

Love leaps the electron gap –
lives flicker, texts fluoresce –
ion traps.

## vi. SOUL-CRADLE

*You're off to Hall. Stone steps:*
*no friend for walking stick and yet*
*you'll smile.*

*Its shield-hung walls. Mitres, earls.*
*Alone among the ranks of men:*
*one bloom.*

I find her in *Godstowe*,
your *Early Rolls,* shadow-robes,
a seal; her faunal shield,
gold-blue. It blazes
on my retina and soothes.

Ela of Warwick. She walks,
distant, by the tangling river.
Centuries flicker, flow.
I can see the rain-does watching,
mist-hung, mauve.

What does she hold?
Charters enrolled
as if she's weaving rushes
for her soul. *Chante pour moi*
she whispers, *chante des prières.*

Our now: her then,
her rustle-hem, her vows
and we in riches,
tatters, 'transhuman',
micro-fetters, genes unspun.

*Lady of the island, Godstowe-grey,*
*grant us a beneficence, Longespée.*

*Ela Longespée, Countess of Warwick* (d.1298) – a founding benefactor of the College (not unlike Elizabeth de Clare, Clare College), she retired to Godstow[e] Abbey, then a fluvial island

## vii. ANNUNCIATION
### Merton College Chapel

*How fire-leaves fray,
colours and college falling away…*

East window, ever-dawn.
It held me once, a pilgrim's pause,
rose, quatrefoils, beckoning.

How it electrified, Virgin and angel
swept in one gold, one green,
as if twin stars or serins.

Anion, cation, invisible exchange.
Such green, meadow-scented,
the College kirtled, sea-lapped

but then – how shadows climb,
how Front Quad clings to cusp,
mouchette, the Virgin annunciate.

Not yet – don't drain the glass
just yet. Mary in her garden,
the angel ever-arriving

*caritas sanctus.* Her dazzled field,
his world-beyond-world.
Light's kiss.

## viii. ÆFENSANG

*Ninety. Your birthday carolled:*
*you glow. How late-found joy*
*can tessellate and grow,*
*a Koch snowflake, fractal.*

Candle-tremor,
crocus tongues.
how notes brush the voussoirs,
soothe and soar.

Beyond, a world too gaunt
to meet alone, Time
in her wolfskin,
siblings shorn.

Cantor to choir, sing on.
*et nunc, et semper, et in saecula.*
The organ's undulations,
*voix celeste,*

choristers frail and beautiful
over the bass,
pale stoles – snow buntings
in flicker-boughs,

spindle-berry robes –
our chaplain a ring ouzel.
Corbel-angels leaning
as if they hear struck icicles

send a pristine shiver
through the stars.

*carolled* – the College choir sang to Roger Highfield on his 90th birthday
*siblings* – Roger sadly lost his parents and elder sister at an early age

## ix. SNOWFLAKES

*So far, so near – to face
the garden, sere. Its
not-yet inflorescence, blossom's gasp.*

Winter's hasp: scents waft
as old leaves lyse. Janus
on the threshold, stone-grey eyes.

Bleak days: your room
is shed. *Its time has passed*
you'd said. White hair, frail shears,

you'd pare, divest, and down
the stairs the fitful snowflakes
came: articles, cuttings,

sloughed skins. *Your door's
grown strange, you are not there –
antonym, cold lozenge.*

Did I pass a Virgil on
the turning stair, letters fading,
numina; a Dante
shelf-worn, lost?

*Janus* – janiform statue in the Fellows' Garden

## x. AMONG THE ARCHIVES

*Stones, stones, the Muniment Room.*
*Your 'Early Rolls' part home.*
*What speaks? A whisper*
*of a whisper, masons' marks.*

Does he sense you,
the young archivist?
Unlocking doors, three-deep
as bell-horizons shudder,
chapel-hauled?

All the lives, lamina:
we're photo-halides,
scrawl; our lees are laid in
glassine, tissue cauls,
clamshell boxes tasting pearls

as if a trace might hold us,
as if a grace might heal us all –
subatomic, spiritual –
our will-o-wisps,
our husks, our

fleeting emanations
and our dust.

*archivist* – Julian Reid

## xi. IN A SLANT OF LIGHT

*A butterfly*
*to support butterflies –*
*a book support, blue foam.*
*It basks on polished tannin,*
*verso, recto, welcomed*
*on each wing.*

It floats in half-light –
Upper Library,
your haven, where folios
nest with faded wings
and roundels bloom
in glass. Outside:
the sun's slow Lazarus.

A glimmer: astrolabes peer,
alidades in unread air.
Do I sense far diamonds
drift, Polaris slip?
Tall books shake their
galley-chains, a blue-swept
globe breathes *salt*...

Such tingling – how photons
bring *Annales* into view;
humidistat, weighing
my breath, wild dew.

*Upper Library* – one of Europe's oldest continuously-used libraries (formerly with chained books), dating from.1378: see Dr Julia Walworth's beautiful *Merton College Library, an Illustrated History* (Bodl. Libr 2020) *astrolabes* – dating from 1350 *globe* (Senex) – c.1740

## xii. THE GARDEN GRACED

*Some lives have icy transoms*
*but not yours. What glasses framed:*
*questing, tacit, warm.*

The sundial sits
on its silent bell, a stone plinth
steeped in loam,

the mulberry stooped,
its walking stick
an echo of your own.

How absences leave hollows.
singing bowls, after-notes
quaking on the rim,

this avenue storm-culled
lime by lime,
Fellows' Garden thinned,

its ache of grass, its
gift of space, of flight –
How the day-star

dances freely, fronds ignite.
Asters, Helianthus –
light within Light.

# EPILOGUE: HANAMI

*Almost a ballet – Grove Garden*
*where Acers float, bokashi,*
*ochre notes, Bi Hō.*

*Japanese cherry pirouettes,*
*rippled, stilled.*

I lived and live it now –
*hanami, umemi –*
no thought of future, past,
only how blossom

breaks, breaks
on the rim of our
abstentions –
all the gardens,

the 'Parks and 'Botanic,
Fellows' and Grove,
petal-mapped,
far Kibworth;

layers, seven heavens,
cherry-pepper anthers,
hairline stems.
Love's silk-screens.

*Grove garden (Merton)* – Japanese plants commemorate Roger Highfield's fond friendship with HIH Crown Prince Naruhito (now installed as Emperor), his pupil 1983–85 – one of the many young minds he would nourish
*Kibworth (Leics)* – Michael Wood's *Story of England* draws on Merton's exquisite archive to bring its long history sensitively to life (BBC 2010, directed Rebecca Dobbs)

# Farm on the Rim

*Devon 2024*

# AS DAWN FEATHERS THE FIELDS
### Three Preludes

i

So fine you'd hardly sense it,
a sky unhusking itself
grey-through-grey.

                          What tingles? We're
                          made of mist and
                          pepper-moths, grisaille.

Ink unlatching from ink,
the farm-hill
hairline, liminal.

                          Slow-fade vowel
                          over our lane,
                          Venusian, cold Lone.

A sparrow's fleeting
circumflex,
blur-winged

                          and through etched trees,
                          striations. Rosolite,
                          fawn-pink.

Beauty learning to speak.
Our hearts
learning to listen.

ii

Last night the tithe-map
talked in my sleep,
*coppice, arable, long furze*
a chant of roods and coulters.
I walked its ink-scratched
acreage and panes, searched
its scattered tesserae
for grain, a tenth of my being
tendered. For a song.

In this morning-before-morning,
sleep paper-thin, I hear
the rags and tatters
of a poem: field-names,
they waft in quarterlight
copper-plate lettering
brushing the grass,
pre-green, pre-rust, earth's
pigments not yet painted.

The *Back'ern* and the *Fallands*,
curve of *Westcott* and *Mr. Pin's*.
*Benjy's Field* and *Little Sood*.
A hay scent: *Brake Linhay*
twitch-ears: *Little Warren*
that riverside eel: *Long Cropley*
and high as our eaves,
the sky's first scarves,
*Home Down*.

If I adopt them, will they
adopt me? Relieve
my frayed impermanence
with their own? Pay out
their silk to swathe our bones,

patchwork cloak
of a borrowed home,
tithe-panes and our soul-wisps
gauged in mommes?

*Forgotten birds,*
*brushed-sandstone made wing,*
*come settle in my*
*vagrant heart and sing.*


iii

What filters, faint, past rafters?
Vanilla hint, cool whey.
Light to cue light.

Hold still: Nick's crates
are dreaming rainbows,
how greys will warm to
purple, cabbage-swirled,
to swede-roots, pungent,
blush-yellow; punnets,
berries, carmine, muscatel.

Hold still: the farm-shop's
sleeping. Henry's planets
wait in rows. Fresh from
the grader, cottage-machine,
he'll float them through –
the sun's a yolk in vitelline,
silver suspension. Fragile.


*mommes* – unit for weighing silk (China)
*grader* – egg-sorting machine

# THIRTY YEARS SINCE
    to my late father

Can it be? So long since you
waded through pewter

a rod and line's
flick-whisper in the flow,

that wake I could not follow
then or now

    *minnow   brook-dun   caddis*
    *mayfly   Donica   dace*

I still can't ford the mystery
between, that place

where murmurs rise from
mallard-green

    *cranefly   yellow-dun   barbel*
    *sedge-fly   Tipula   eel*

though inner life will quicken,
rill by rill

as if these flickers link us.
Wandering; still.

# VULPINE

Glancing up from suds, tea-plate's
humble horizon, I freeze
to see three-feet of flame
sashay under my window

startling in December sunlight –
not ochre, heartbeat, haw, but all
as if her burning instant
gives them life.

Here she lives by her own law
pacing supple rings of fire.
This rag-rug we think ours is hers

for who else opens
the gates of the sun?

# FOR THE SUBPOSTMASTERS
   i.m. of Christow, Lynton & Bishops Tawton post offices (Devon)

Not that you'd see him at first,
moth-flutter hands busy,
the curve of his cheek,
a shy moon; and then – a shift
of cardigan – his glance
through glass, warm as
garnet-schist, tea's rush.

He's here for us, for this
lad running in – *change
a fiver, mate?* – this
slip-of-a-woman, arms thin
as a wishbone-bird, her
bag on wheels, a bell's
tiny blessing over her head.

He's tins, aspirin, elastic bands,
*eggs? Sue brought them
this morning,* while grocer's gone,
library-van. Not that regents
will hear us, wielding their shears
top-down, who'd pare
our lives to rootstock,

put pixels in his place
and furnish us with nothing –
Touchless touchscreens.
Faceless 'face'.

# NEWBORN

She is not a barcode,
not a QR code,
she was born
for face to face, not screen.

Must you estrange her
from herself?
Swathe her in 'sensors',
track, surveil her

microchip
and microwave her,
abuse, un-birth,
blaspheme?

Look: her eyes are jewels –
roe-lit, hazel,
leaf-lamp, sky –
bright pools,

all you might miss.
She's beauty born for
beauty. Bliss.
Not this strange shell, not this.

---

*microwave* – everyday wireless technologies; for toxicology see e.g. my colleague D J Panagopoulos, PhD, ed., *Electromagnetic Fields of Wireless Communications: Biological and Health Effects*, Routledge 2023

# A QUEST FOR SUNLIGHT
### East Hill

Ever my love, elusive sun,
taking your gift, your
saffron song to the rim.

I search for you
through silhouettes,
consonants of ash and thorn,
waiting for your
yellow vowel to flower.

Pollen-tint, where are you?
Picogram in weightless air,
mica's glint, ochre's glow,
turmeric's stray dust.

Ever my love, I seek you
where path-rocks bloom and grow,
where streaks of light
flick through the trees

yes no,
yes no,
yes no

# A PRAYER FOR LOST GARDENS

Snowdrop
as you bow your head
whisper it – only whisper it –

earth cannot bear
more shouts of war, gun-shot,
heart-quake, shatterings –

whisper your prayer
to broken ground, dust
made cist, lintels mist, Raqqa,
Tigray, Khan Younis,

a slip of light from
indelible Light

garden
to lost gardens.

*Raqqa…* – Syria, Ethiopia, Gaza, to name but a few

# ORION AT THE DOORWAY

*Aren't you worried, living out there,*
*cycling in the dark?*
But it's not far, not lone:
we've hedge sparrows
and sometimes a stock-boy
freckles the hill
a head-torch for a star;

not far, I'm not John Clare
trudging home from Ryhall,
a sholt and suther
through unmarked miles
though starlings scrawl
in tree-frets and sea-winds
trail wild voices, rake our creel.

It's not far, this rattle-shell,
slipper limpet in stellar flows,
Orion at the front door,
Plough at the back:
old friends, how could I
abandon them for halogens,
pan-digital skin?

And the Seven Stars ask
*what light have you sewn?*
and the Hunter asks
*what shadows have you slain?*
as they hang there, dripping
diamonds, delicate fire,
as if the shiver of the universe

is our crucible,
our home.

## ALL THE DROWNED BIRDS

One by one, we'll lose them
to black holes

as they slope onto the bus –
gosling or farouche,

freckled or belle,
young lives caught in a long farewell

as they fidget, teeter, fall –
wings pinned, necks bent –

in a four-inch pool
to scroll, glaze over, scroll

all the drowned birds

while trees, unloved, sway by,
hills, bereaved

all guests in my eyes,
fieldscape and sky –

> *Leaf-light, miraculous,*
> *Fresh hay, strawberry-blond.*
> *Rust-blue, a jay's revelation,*

# OUT OF THE SKY

We wake to snowfall, slow-motion, hypnotic,
a bright poem falling out of the sky
like god sleeting through the world

and time dissolving. Fibre-glass falling
on roof-tree and wall, ash-branch and bole,
glacial in each leaf's valley

as mercury floats on zero and short days
utter ice. Hexagons, no two the same,
white words that will never be spoken again.

We watch their crystals haunt and glow
and for one breath I see our lives
as burning, brief, improbable as snow.

## TWO BUZZARDS
   for Ian

Tiny under high cloud,
they dance
their casual ballet-of-beyond,
miles spinning under them,
copses, sheds,
frail pathways.

I watch from the dropped
tatami of our garden,
kelim to carry us
as they meet and part,
meet and part,
riding wide rings

like the circles
I sometimes trace with you,
life linked to life,
circumferences, cobalt,
growing, as if our love
makes portals in the blue

but the birds gather
distance, mystery,
black binaries
in a growing sky,
roofs and tillage falling away,
frittered page

under the deft dismissal
of their wings.

# ROBBIE'S VIOLETS
   Devon 2023–2024

Fuel costs, feed costs,
drought-stress and storm

when all his world turned brown
then churned with rain

the headland-field a prow
lifting, dipping,

fading angels over the sea,
unreadable light

on their wings
as news, knife-wind, ushers

yet here they are – violets –
more profuse than ever

their scented wells,
salving dyes, night's eyebath

as if an Eden rises
in us yet.